Pathfinder 21

A CILT series for language teachers

Creative use of texts

Bernard Kavanagh and Lynne Upton

CiLT

Other titles in the PATHFINDER series:

Reading for pleasure in a foreign language (Ann Swarbrick)
Communication re-activated: teaching pupils with learning difficulties
    (Bernardette Holmes)
Yes - but will they behave? Managing the interactive classroom
    (Susan Halliwell)
On target - teaching in the target language (Susan Halliwell and Barry Jones)
Bridging the gap: GCSE to 'A' level (John Thorogood and Lid King)
Making the case for languages (Alan Moys and Richard Townsend)
Languages home and away (Alison Taylor)
Being creative (Barry Jones)
Departmental planning and schemes of work (Clive Hurren)
Progressing through the Attainment Targets (Ian Lane)
Continuous assessment and recording (John Thorogood)
Fair enough? Equal opportunities and modern languages (Vee Harris)
Improve your image: the effective use of the OHP
    (Daniel Tierney and Fay Humphreys)
Not bothered? Motivating reluctant learners in Key Stage 4
    (Jenifer Alison)
Grammar matters (Susan Halliwell)
Differentiation (Anne Convery and Do Coyle)
Drama in the languages classroom (Judith Hamilton and Anne McLeod)
Nightshift - ideas and strategies for homework
    (David Buckland and Mike Short)

First published 1994
Copyright © 1994 Centre for Information on Language Teaching and Research
ISBN 1 874016 28 3

Cover by Logos Design & Advertising
Printed in Great Britain by Oakdale Printing Co. Ltd.

Published by the Centre for Information on Language Teaching and Research,
20 Bedfordbury, Covent Garden, London WC2N 4LB.

Contents

Exploiting a text: some practical suggestions for:

Introduction

We all use written texts in our classroom, from script written on a board to reading schemes and authentic documents. This book looks at a number of approaches which have been used in schools and colleges, to help you to enrich your range of activities with text. We provide many examples, but our aim is to bring out the principles underlying each of them, so that you can find or devise materials which suit your own learners and situations.

The book deals with two kinds of creativity: the teacher's and the learner's. It suggests ways in which you can vary your uses of text and ways in which your pupils can be helped to use text as a springboard for making language their own. We see the book as being complementary to *Being creative* by Barry Jones (CILT, 1992), which focuses on classroom atmosphere and teacher attitude, and provides a panoply of creative activities.

In the definitions given in *Modern Foreign Languages in the National Curriculum* (DES, 1991), emphasis is placed on **responses** to the written word as against testing. Language skills are interdependent, both in pupil learning and in real-life language use; our aim in this book is to examine ways in which text can reinforce and extend what pupils are learning to say and write.

The approaches suggested have all been tried and tested in class, from year 7 to year 13 (and beyond), and many were presented at a CILT Conference on *Creativity and the school language learner*.

1. Text and pronunciation

Pupils who are learning European languages which have an alphabet similar to that of their native language need to 'learn the system', so that they are less likely to confuse, in French *demain/semaine* or in German *dien* and *dein* and so on. It is a common occurrence in classrooms to see students attempting to write words in a foreign language, but using the system of their native language (*Wee, Musher* and the like). It may well be that we don't spend enough time helping them grapple with the system of the foreign language, that is, representing sounds in writing. As recommended in the Programmes of Study, Part 1, *Modern Foreign Languages in the National Curriculum* (1991):

> *Students should have regular opportunities to learn how sounds are represented in writing* and to *develop their awareness of the different conventions of the written and spoken language.*

The following activities focus on the way in which sounds are represented in writing in French.

DESTINATIONS

Pupils match passengers to destinations which rhyme with their names.

Monsieur Hari va à Paris ... où vont les autres?

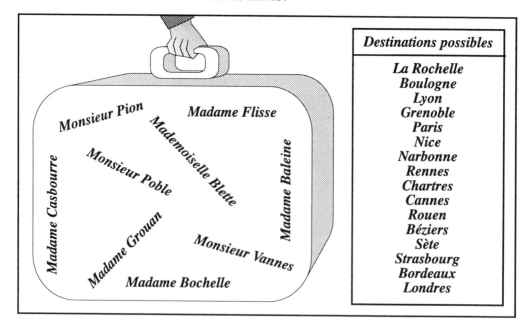

Destinations possibles

- *La Rochelle*
- *Boulogne*
- *Lyon*
- *Grenoble*
- *Paris*
- *Nice*
- *Narbonne*
- *Rennes*
- *Chartres*
- *Cannes*
- *Rouen*
- *Béziers*
- *Sète*
- *Strasbourg*
- *Bordeaux*
- *Londres*

Passengers:
Monsieur Pion, *Madame Flisse*, *Mademoiselle Blette*, *Madame Baleine*, *Madame Casbourre*, *Monsieur Poble*, *Madame Grouan*, *Monsieur Vannes*, *Madame Bochelle*

Note that there are more destinations than there are travellers; this means that the learner has a larger field from which to choose, so that the last example is not solved simply by elimination of all others.

If the class is now provided with another list of surnames, real or fictitious, and a map of France, they could be invited to find destinations of which the last syllable might rhyme with the last syllable of the names. *Monsieur Seille, Madame Rance, Mademoiselle Flan* might respectively be on their way to Marseille, Valence and Le Mans, while *Madame Bonbec* and *Monsieur Bréal* are possibly bound for Canada.

We are not, of course, suggesting that teaching should be **based** on such 'revelation' of systems, but just as grammatical patterns are taught when the need for them is clear, and when the learner has already had experience of them, so other systems can usefully be taught - in whole or in part. Primary school teachers spend a lot of time helping pupils to recognise the sounds letters make, in combination. We need to do more of this in teaching a foreign language, especially for those who find reading in their own language difficult.

Variation
- In a similar way, pupils could pair off teachers and their subjects: *Monsieur Platte enseigne les maths, Madame Morlaix l'anglais, Mademoiselle Vaillant l'allemand,* etc.

A POEM

In the early years we might teach little poems, such as *Le ballon*, to show pupils how internal rhymes work.

This poem is to be found in *99 poèmes, 9 contes, 9 comptines, choisis par Pomme d'Api,* published by Editions Bayars, 1992; many others of this kind are available in materials devised for the *Ecole Maternelle.*

Le ballon

Julien le tient,
Mathieu le veut,
Roland le prend,
Constance le lance,
Agathe le rate,
Paf! Il éclate.

Qu'est-ce qui cloche?

Other activities which draw attention to sound and script might include these:

- Given a number of words (six or eight), pupils spot the odd one out: *plat, la, grenat, fat, gras, masse, extra, bas.*
- Given a number of words (six or eight at a time), pupils might be invited to pair them off: *pin, Martine, Martin, vlan, Christine, allemand.*

It is clear that such activities are most relevant in French, because it is particularly difficult phonetically. In German, there are similar, but less acute, problems for the learner. In Italian and Spanish they are minimal.

Un petit commerçant

As a last example, here is a piece of work on 'comparative code', suitable for year 9. Pupils have to put themselves in the shoes of a French speaker who has little English and who represents English words according to French 'rules'. Having read an account of how a French shopkeeper learned an English word, learners are asked which English words he might hear in those given below.

La semaine dernière, un touriste anglais est rentré chez nous et m'a demandé du 'ouaïne'. Je n'ai rien compris. Il a continué à répéter 'ouaïne', 'ouaïne'. Je lui ai montré du fromage: ce n'était pas cela - ils disent 'chiz'; du café? Non, cela, c'était du 'cofi'...

Enfin, il a vu, derrière moi, une rangée de bouteilles de vin et d'apéritifs. 'Zere you are', m'a-t-il dit, 'ouaïne!' Je lui ai vendu une douzaine de bouteilles de vin rouge. Et j'ai appris un mot anglais très utile: 'ouaïne'!

- *Quels sont les mots anglais représentés?*

amme	*vinigueux*	*ouette-fiche*	*praïce*	*mite*
bouque	*achetré*	*pronnecoquetelle*	*basquitte*	*ammebague*
tchiquinne	*tchocleute*	*ouinedeau*		

Adapted from *Pigé!*, Book 3 (Nelson).

Having done this exercise, could students invent a few of their own? (*corquescrou? paquitte? panne?*)

2. Text and talking

Much work has been done to find ways of helping learners to talk to each other in the target language, exchanging genuinely needed information. Cue cards are common practice, as are questionnaires. We have been rather more reluctant to use **text** as a springboard for talk, fearing perhaps that this might make for difficulties of comprehension, or for 'lifting' answers wholesale. All the tasks and activities which follow have been tried in class. We have found that if pupils are led carefully through graded texts and tasks, the use of text is a rich addition to their diet. The activities also provide some useful pointers for creating assessment tasks where the response is in the target language, or in symbols.

We assume that pupils have been learning to exchange personal details, preferably using fictional identities, so that their 'personal details' are not always the same: they might be Marcel Plon, aged 16, with three brothers and no sisters, living in a flat with his parents, interested in computing and football; or they might become Michel Duval, aged 14, with a brother and sister, living in a house on the outskirts of Paris, interested in rock-climbing and basketball... and so on.

CUE CARDS

Pupils make a cue card in notes/symbols, which they then use as stimulus for talk. You might start them off like this:

> *Tu lis le texte et tu notes les informations sous forme de symboles:*
>
> *Son nom est Pascal Leblanc. Il habite à Rouen. Il a un frère qui s'appelle Jérôme et qui a cinq ans. Il habite avec ses parents, et Jérôme, dans un appartement.*

This results in this kind of cue card:

During their reading, pupils can have access to help from a variety of reference works, including dictionaries (if available), to overcome any problems of comprehension.

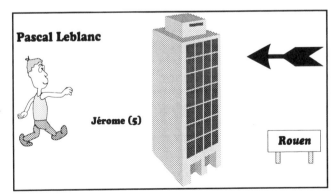

The cue cards - covering a range of identities - can now be used as a basis for interviews and the following sequence of activities can be carried out:

● each pupil notes in symbol form the information obtained from 'interviewees';
● each uses the symbols to write a third person 'report';
● pupils now compare this 'report' with the paragraph which their partner began with.

This last stage allows pupils to see those features which distinguish their own work from the original; what better way to learn how written reports differ in style from dialogues, and how to link ideas in writing?

DETECTIVE WORK

This activity uses a similar technique but takes on aspects of a game which involves role play, questioning and reading. The class has to discover which one of (say) three possible characters matches in every detail a given 'portrait'.

This is how it works.

● All the class can see (on paper, OHT or board) a text like this one, which describes the character they are to seek:

Texte de base

Amélie Durand est une fille de 12 ans. Elle habite à Colmar, en Alsace, dans une villa. Elle n'a ni frères ni sœurs. Elle a un chat du nom de Minuscule (c'est un tout petit chat); il est gris. Amélie aime bien le collège. En particulier, elle aime les mathématiques. Son anniversaire, c'est le deux mai.
    Trois filles prétendent être la vraie Amélie Durand. Questionnez-les pour découvrir laquelle est la véritable Amélie.

● Three pupils play the roles of the three 'pretenders' - only one of them is of course the 'real' Amélie. Their 'identities' are given to them on the following cards:

Ton nom est Amélie Durand.   **A**
Tu aimes bien le collège; ta matière préférée, c'est les mathématiques.
Tu es fille unique.
Tu habites à Colmar, en Alsace, dans une villa.
Tu as un chat du nom de Minuscule - il est tout petit, et gris.
Ton anniversaire, c'est le deux mai.

Tu t'appelles Amélie Durand.
Tu es fille unique.
Tu as douze ans - ton anniversaire, c'est le deux mai.
Tu habites à Colmar, en Alsace, dans un appartement.
Tu as un petit chat gris du nom de Minuscule.
Tu aimes bien le collège; les mathématiques, voilà ta matière préférée.

Ton nom est Amélie Durand. Tu n'as ni frères ni soeurs.
Tu habites une villa, à Colmar, en Alsace.
Tu as douze ans - ton anniversaire, c'est le deux mai.
Ton petit chat est gris; il s'appelle Minuscule.
Tu aimes bien le collège.
Ta matière préférée, c'est le français.

- The class now interviews the three 'pretenders' to find which of them is the real Amélie Durand.

- Each pupil makes notes, perhaps on a grid provided or on one devised by themselves, of the answers received.

- When someone is quite sure that the person sought has been identified, he or she says so and indicates, in the target language, which piece of information has been the determining one.

A few notes.

- If pupils do not record answers, they are quite likely to ask for information they already have. Often, they ask the questions without addressing them to one of the trio, and are surprised when either no-one answers, or all three do - in unison! These occurrences are interesting in themselves; more importantly, though, the eyes of the majority of the pupils can be seen reading (scanning) the *texte de base* over and over again. Each member of the trio, similarly, reads and re-reads his or her text.

- As can be seen by comparing the first text and the second, it is easy to vary both the order in which information is given and also the layout of the text on the page; having the information on separate lines helps the less able.

- In writing the texts, do not place the information which gives the game away in the same place in each text.

- The 'character' texts need not of course be written with as many variations in the language used.

- The three 'characters' could be given their texts quite a time in advance, and invited to make notes or to encode the details in the symbols they are already used to employing.

- Take care that all relevant information is given in each text, so that pupils are not left stranded when asked a certain question. Similarly, make sure that the interrogators know clearly which 'fields' are relevant, i.e. that they do not ask Amélie about her friends, or her favourite music.

- If you provide a grid, set it out so that it does not encourage the class to ask too early those questions which reveal the identity they seek.

Variations
- Once the conventions are accepted, a number of variations are possible, with different topics, e.g. reporting/narrating recent events, where three (or more) accounts of an evening are given and one of the characters is 'lying'.

STAGE-DIRECTED DIALOGUE

Written dialogues, as well as descriptive or narrative texts, can be used as a springboard for different kinds of talk. When you have been teaching a class to 'make arrangements to go out together' - suggesting, accepting, asking about details, refusing, giving reasons/pretexts, making alternative proposals, agreeing, arranging a time and place to meet, for instance - there are uses for written versions of the dialogues, as well as ones they hear.

Whether heard or read, such a dialogue might have the following shape:

Jacques *Si on allait à la piscine?*
Jean *Ah, non! Je n'ai pas envie de me baigner.*
Jacques *Alors, qu'est-ce que tu veux faire?*
Jean *Je voudrais bien aller au ciné: il y a un bon film à l'Odéon.*
Jacques *OK, d'accord.*
Jean *Tu viens chez moi?*
Jacques *Non, je n'aurai pas le temps.*
Jean *D'accord. Devant le cinéma, alors? A neuf heures moins le quart?*
Jacques *Bien. A tout à l'heure.*

Presenting a framework with 'stage directions' could now help pupils to recall the text - another aid to acquiring the relevant language. It might look like this:

Jacques *(propose la piscine)*
Jean *(refuse absolument)*

Jacques	*(invite autre proposition)*
Jean	*(propose le cinéma)*
Jacques	*(accepte)*
Jean	*(propose rendez-vous)*
Jacques	*(refuse, donne raison)*
Jean	*(propose autre rendez-vous et heure)*
Jacques	*(accepte)*

Not only can this be an *aide-mémoire*, it can also be used more creatively, since the utterances given in the 'model' dialogue are by no means the only possible ones. At a second stage, we might invite the class to suggest alternative language. For '*propose la piscine*' they might offer:

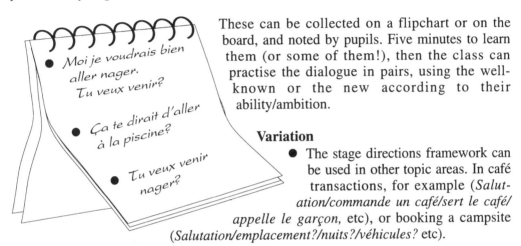

These can be collected on a flipchart or on the board, and noted by pupils. Five minutes to learn them (or some of them!), then the class can practise the dialogue in pairs, using the well-known or the new according to their ability/ambition.

Variation

- The stage directions framework can be used in other topic areas. In café transactions, for example (*Salutation/commande un café/sert le café/appelle le garçon*, etc), or booking a campsite (*Salutation/emplacement?/nuits?/véhicules?* etc).

DIALOGUE WITH AN EMOTIONAL CHARGE

GCSE and other materials can lead to a great deal of transactional language. Our pupils have welcomed the chance to work with dialogues in which there is some kind of emotional involvement on the part of the speakers. They recognise both the situations and the emotions, from their own experience.

One approach would be as follows. Pupil volunteers read the dialogue in so far as it is provided. Where there is only a stage direction, the class is invited to 'find' something appropriate. The teacher lists the suggestions where all can see (correcting as necessary), as in the previous example. When the end of the dialogue is reached, other pairs of readers can give their version of it, choosing from among the collection of *répliques* listed.

Julien	*Allô. Ici Julien.*
Annie	*Bonjour, Julien.*

Julien	*Dis, tu veux aller au ciné ce soir?*
Annie	*(indifférente)*
Julien	*Bon, alors, tu veux faire autre chose?*
Annie	*(hésite)*
Julien	*(avec impatience)*
Annie	*(se décide) OK, écoute: c'est que j'ai de nouveaux patins. J'aimerais bien aller patiner.*
Julien	*(hésite) Mais... mais... je ne sais pas patiner, moi.*
Annie	*(enthousiaste)*
Julien	*(se laisse persuader)*

CLASSIFICATION

It can be helpful to learners to revise some of the language they have been learning by arranging utterances according to their functions, e.g. how many ways do I know of suggesting an activity, or refusing someone else's suggestions?

The class uses a grid like the one below and, together or in groups, fills the columns with possible language items:

Propose	Accepte	Refuse	Raison	Rendez-vous où/quand	
Tu veux... ?	*Oui.*	*Non.*	*Je fais du*	*Chez moi.*	*17h*
Si on allait... ?	*Je veux bien.*	*Je n'ai pas*	*baby-sitting.*	*Chez toi.*	*18h30*
J'ai envie de...	*OK.*	*envie*	*Je ne sais pas...*	*Devant*	*20h30*
Et toi?			*Je n'ai pas d'argent.*	*le cinéma.*	

As these suggestions are collected, you may wish to add more examples in some or all of the columns; this will depend on the ability and keenness of the group. Selectively, the contents of the table can be covered up, rubbed out, revealed, to encourage pupils to recall the missing elements - an aid to learning. Some pupils may want to note down all or part of the table for reference purposes.

This might be an occasion, too, for presenting to the class some language which belongs to another register, e.g. the formal register, by introducing expressions such as *Est-ce que vous seriez libre vendredi, par hasard?* or *Je regrette, je suis pris ce soir.* Ask students to speculate when such utterances might be appropriate. This provides them with a glimpse into the notion of register.

NARRATION

Pupils use written accounts of events as a springboard to asking questions and giving information, with the help of a framework. As a first step, they can be taught question forms for interviewing their partner about an 'event' (*fait divers*, *accident*, etc). For example:

C'est un accident?/vol?
Il y a combien de personnes?
Quel temps faisait-il?
L'incident s'est passé où?
Qu'est-ce qui s'est passé d'abord?

Et ensuite?
Et après?
Qu'est-ce qui a provoqué l'incident?
Et les conséquences?

Just as the stage directions in previous examples acted as reminders of a range of things to say, a grid with headings could prompt these questions. It might look like this:

Having practised asking and answering this range of questions with familiar material, pupils can now be asked to put them to use with less familiar material:

- Half the class has the grid, the other half an account; those with the grid find out what happened.
- The same operation, but in pairs.
- At the end of either activity the information seekers can produce an oral or written summary from their notes.

Contexte:

Moment:
(saison, temps, heure) ◯

Participants:

Suite des événements:
(d'abord, puis, ensuite...)

Causes: ◯

Conséquences:

Variations

- Take a longer, but clearly sequenced text, and divide it so that no-one has the whole story. Best if the sections correspond roughly to the headings on the grid.

- With advanced level students, divide in two each of a number of 'human interest' stories such as can be found in 'News in Brief' sections of local newspapers. Mark the first half of each with A and the second with B.
  - Ask a student with an A card to summarise his or her text.
  - The others scan their text to see whether they have the second half. When found, this is in turn summarised.
  - All the other members of the class make notes on what they hear. If they write an account from their notes, they can then compare their writing with the original article.

3.   Reading to learn

We are asked by the National Curriculum Order to ensure that pupils have access to a programme of graded texts on a variety of subjects and in a variety of styles likely to catch their interest (see Statements of Attainment, Attainment Target 3). An excellent account of how to set up a pupil reading scheme, ideas for student and teacher record-keeping, and ways of helping pupils to see how they can learn language from their reading are all contained in *Reading for pleasure* by Ann Swarbrick (CILT, 1990).

The Order also says that learners' competence in reading (as in listening) is to be tested in the target language, except where it is necessary to use another language, for example, in an interpretation activity. So we need to move away from such exercises as 'true/false statements', which do not always tell us what the learner can do, and are unlikely in themselves to give rise to much language acquisition.

In this section, we look at these two issues:

- strategies for helping pupils to learn language through reading, by motivating them to read texts attentively and more than once;
- assessment in the target language, or at least in ways other than using English.

Language teachers know that for learners to acquire a new word, they need to hear it in context a number of times (four? six? eight?), maybe to see it written, and to repeat it to themselves. As learners, we all know how lucky we are if a word 'sticks' immediately, and (even more importantly) permanently. If reading activities are to yield dividends in terms of language acquired, several conditions need to prevail.

- The text needs to be of interest, either intrinsically (i.e. pupils might well wish to read it if they were native speakers of the target language), or as a clear reinforcement of language they have been learning elsewhere, so that they see the 'pay-off'.

- The text needs to be accessible, so that the learner is not obliged to 'look up' every other word, though it can - and often should - contain elements which are unknown to the pupils, as is required at Level 4 onwards of AT3.

- The task needs to require the learners to read the text with care, a number of times, and it needs to appeal to them as a task.

- Learners need a variety of tasks as well as of texts.

- Tasks as well as texts will need to be differentiated to match a range of abilities.

- Learners need to be equipped with strategies for dealing with the unknown.

TRANSCODING

A simple task with a response in the target language or in symbols is one which requires pupils to take pieces of information from a text and enter these on a grid under relevant headings. We have mentioned this already in the chapter on reading and talking, where students made cue cards from written reports (p 5). If texts and tasks are as simple as in the following example, the activity runs the risk of being mechanical: all the relevant information is given, in the same order as in the grid headings, and there is little to intrigue the reader.

Hallo. Ich bin Kristina. Ich bin zwölf. Ich wohne mit meinen Eltern in einer Wohnung, in Rodenkirchen.
Name: **Haustyp**
Alter: **Heimatstadt:**

However, if we make the exercise a little more demanding, the fact that pupils have done a number of such simple transcodings will have been good preparation.

Here, the headings in the grid are not in the same order as the information in the text, in which there is also considerable redundancy. It is easy to see that a sequence of such texts could be found in textbooks or magazines, or they could be home-produced; and the language will reinforce some of the things pupils are trying to say.

Guten Tag. Mein Name ist Friedrich und ich bin elf. Ich komme aus Österreich: ich bin in Wien geboren und wohne jetzt in Linz. Mein Bruder heißt Georg. Ich habe keine Schwester. Mein Vater ist Briefträger und meine Mutter ist Lehrerin.
Name: **Geburtsort:**
Alter: **Geschwister:**
Wohnort:

'CHARACTER' TEXTS

With a little imagination, we can present the learners with the unexpected, and they can take pleasure in the success of dealing with it. Consider, for example, the following set of paragraphs, all on a common theme:

1. *Marie Leclerc a dix ans. Elle habite Rungis. Elle a deux frères et une sœur. Elle partage sa chambre avec sa sœur, qui s'appelle Eliane.*

2. *Paul Duval a douze ans. Il habite près de Dieppe. Il a deux sœurs et un frère. Il partage une chambre avec son petit frère Jean-Luc, qui a deux ans. Paul n'aime pas cela.*

3. *Guillaume habite un château près de Dijon. Dans le château il y a seize chambres et huit salles de bains. Dans sa chambre, Guillaume a un téléviseur, une chaîne hi-fi, un ordinateur et un train électrique: il a sept ans.*

4. *Frédéric partage son lit avec Globule. Frédéric est un gros chien noir, et Globule, c'est un petit chat gris. Ils habitent chez Monsieur Plon, dans le garage.*

From the 'flat' text about Marie Leclerc, the pupil moves to the paragraph on Paul Duval; here, with minimal change, the text takes on an emotional colour, in that he does not like sharing his bedroom with a two-year-old, a feeling which year 7 children will know. The third text adds the idea of a spoilt child; and then there are Frédéric (Who is this person who shares a bed with someone with an outlandish name?) and Globule to consider. The last three texts, then, have elements of character, which increases their appeal.

The above texts have probably required more than one reading. In the following activities, the pupil will certainly need to read the texts attentively a number of times.

SPOT THE DIFFERENCE

An activity which requires careful reading of the information given in two or more accounts. It could be something like this:

Deux élèves parlent de leur amie Claudine; ils ne sont pas toujours d'accord sur les détails. Tu notes les différences, e.g. Paul dit: Claudine a un petit chien; Michel dit: Elle a un gros chien, etc.

Michel: *J'aime bien Claudine. Elle adore la natation, et moi aussi. Elle habite au 12 rue de la Gare, près de chez moi. Elle a un petit chien noir, et un chat gris. Le chien s'appelle Mitterrand et le chat, Vas-y. La sœur de Claudine s'appelle Gabrielle.*

Paul: *Claudine est une de mes amies. Elle a douze ans. Elle habite au quatorze, rue de la Gare, près de chez Michel. Elle aime les animaux: son gros chien noir s'appelle Président et son chat, Vas-y. Vas-y est gris. Elle a une sœur du nom de Gabriella. Claudine aime bien aller à la piscine.*

It is worth noting (and pupils would need warning of this) that the differences we are looking for are to do with information and not with the way in which things are expressed. Readers need to spot that although Michel does not mention the swimming bath, only the abstract *natation*, both boys make the same point: Claudine likes to swim. The intention is, indeed, that pupils should learn that there are legitimate variants on what they have already learned, and so enrich their stock of language.

At a more advanced level, such an activity could take the form of non-congruent accounts of childhood memories, or a discussion where students spot the main differences between the views expressed by writers or speakers.

Variation
● A mirror image of 'Spot the difference' is 'What do they have in common?', where pupils must spot a common factor in a set of texts (all three might mention a girl called Mary, Marie, Maria; all might contain references to capital cities, or all allude to sets of twins...).

MATCHING

There are many possibilities here; the essence is that pupils, given one set of information, search in another source to make the best match. Although best done using a database on a computer, such activities can also be done as a paper exercise.

● Pupils read paragraphs about Paul, Jack and Bill, which provide information about their age, size, tastes in music and sport. They then search a database for the best match with potential Spanish penfriends.

● Pupils read portraits of a number of boys and match them with potential blind dates from details of girls given in a database.

● Pupils read letters in which potential customers state their preferences for hotel accommodation and search a database with details of hotels in a given area to find the best match.

ATTRIBUTION OF UTTERANCES

A useful variation on the same theme. Here learners are presented with information on a number of people (personal details, character traits, tics, interests, likes, dislikes, talents, deficiencies...), and a number of utterances. The task is to match each utterance to one of the people characterised in the reports.

> *Philippe habite Lausanne. Il a douze ans. Son père est suisse, sa mère est d'origine anglaise. Philippe a la chance d'être bilingue.*
>
> *Denise habite Bruxelles. Ella a quatorze ans. Toute la famille parle flamand comme langue maternelle, et ils parlent français aussi.*
>
> *Rakesh habite Leicester. Il parle gujerati et anglais. Au collège, tous les cours sont donnés en anglais (sauf les classes de français, bien entendu!). C'est dans la cour que Rakesh et ses amis parlent gujerati de temps en temps.*
>
> *Qui a dit...?*
> *(a) Oui, j'habite en Belgique.*
> *(b) J'habite une ville dans les Midlands.*
> *(c) On ne parle français que dans les cours de français.*
> *(d) Maman est d'origine britannique.*

At a more advanced level, you might challenge the reader to infer as well as simply match, e.g. if Georges is said to be two years older than his brother, whose age is given as twelve, then it will be Georges who said *Moi, j'ai quatorze ans*. That is a simple piece of arithmetic. More demandingly, the problem might have a cultural dimension, e.g. if someone called Denise is said to like pop but not classical music, the utterance *Je suis allée au concert: on a joué du Ravel* is unlikely to be hers...

Alternatively, pupils can be given a number of statements and asked to say which remark matches which statement, e.g.:

> *Was lernen sie gern?*
> *Marion mag Mathe; sie mag Fremdsprachen nicht.*
> *Alfred mag Mathe nicht; sein Lieblingsfach ist Erdkunde.*
> *Michael mag Französisch; Deutsch aber mag er nicht.*
> *Olga mag Englisch, aber ihr Lieblingsfach ist Deutsch.*
>
> *Bemerkungen*
> *1. Er mag Fremdsprachen.*
> *2. Sie mag Deutsch.*
> *3. Sie mag Französisch nicht.*
> *4. Sie findet Mathe interessant.*
> *5. Erdkunde ist sein Lieblingsfach.*

PUZZLES

It is possible to add to such activities an even more overt 'puzzle' dimension, for example:

SPOT THE NONSENSE

Here students are invited to read and re-read text in order to see whether it makes sense and, if it doesn't, state why not. Note that the errors are not linguistic, but to do with textual coherence or non-correspondence to real life. For instance, the writer might say *Je suis fille unique* and then go on to talk of her brothers. In the second category would be such statements as *Mon professeur de français a douze ans.*

WHO'S WHO?

This example takes up the practice of entering information on to a grid, but gives it a twist.

Il y a trois enfants, Annique, Anne et Agnès.   *Tu remplis la grille avec leurs détails personnels:*

Prénom	Age	Domicile	Maison/appartement

La fille qui habite Rouen a douze ans.
La fille qui habite la banlieue de Paris a onze ans.
La fille qui a onze ans habite un appartement.
La fille qui habite à Nice a huit ans.
La fille qui a douze ans habite une maison.

La fille qui a huit ans habite une maison.
Anne et Agnès habitent des maisons.
Anne a douze ans.
Annique n'habite pas au bord de la mer.
Agnès n'habite pas Paris.

It is as well, with children of average ability, to emphasise that there are in fact only three children to contend with, not ten or more!

What do pupils have to do to complete this task successfully? They must take meaning into account, and also do a little deduction. Of course, it is possible, on reading the first of the ten statements, to enter something on to the grid (under *Domicile* we can write Rouen and under *Age,* 12). But the names cannot be deduced and entered in this mechanical way: the nettle of the last few statements has eventually to be grasped.

It is true that some children are more intrigued than others by such exercises in elementary logic, and that an unrelieved diet of such puzzles would in any case soon pall; however, they do present to those who are not so good at absorbing language, but good at deduction, the chance to shine. And not all such activities need to be done individually - they can equally well be done in pairs, or threes, or as whole-class activities.

With or without the puzzle dimension, all these activities have outcomes which are (if they are in a language at all) in the target language and this is a great gain, in National Curriculum terms.

Admittedly, they are not practical, real-life activities; but attempts to ensure the latter have in the past led to some unlikely examination rubrics, haven't they? (e.g. You are in France and your penfriend suggests a visit to the zoo; make a list, in French [!!!], of ten animals you want to remember to look at.) We should want to argue that what you lose in apparent validity you gain in usefulness!

The fact that the response is not in English and that it does not risk being obscured by lack of competence in writing in the target language is common also to the following activities. Only time will show how far it is really possible, as the National Curriculum requires, to test reading competence reliably without recourse to English.

READING AND DRAWING

Give pupils a written text which is a description - of a cartoon, say, or some other uncluttered picture - and then ask them to draw as much of it as they can. This fulfils the two conditions set out earlier: multiple reading and an outcome which is not in English.

Variations
● Given three short written descriptions and one picture, decide which text matches the picture exactly.

● Given stage directions for the first scene of a play, draw the stage as described; Ionesco's *Rhinoceros* is a good play for this, or you can write or commission your own from the assistant. A variant can be to provide some of the information on audio tape, as if on the radio, and complementary information in written text.

Two hints:

● Make sure that it is possible to complete the drawing without having to rub out bits because the details are modified subsequently. Try it out on a colleague first.

● Make sure that the orientation is clear, e.g. does 'to the right of Mrs Jones' mean as we see it, or as she sees it? Again, pilot the task before letting the class loose on it.

MAPPING

Pupils read a descriptive or narrative text and mark on a prepared map the path taken by the narrator or a character.

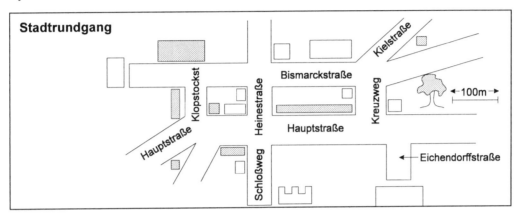

Here the student uses the map given to follow the route outlined in the text; the unshaded buildings are to be identified:

Ich wohne in einer kleinen Wohnung im Schloßweg. Dies ist eine Sackgasse. Am Ende des Schloßwegs steht das alte Schloß. Heutzutage ist das nur noch eine Ruine. Am anderen Ende der Straße ist die Hauptstraße. Dort gibt es viele Geschäfte. An der Ecke der Hauptstraße und der Heinestraße steht das Rathaus. Es ist eines der größten und der ältesten Gebäude der Stadt. Am anderen Ende der Heinestraße ist die Post. Nach der Post kommt man zur Bismarckstraße. Links (etwa 200 Meter) liegt der Hauptbahnhof und rechts, an der Ecke der Kielstraße und der Bismarckstraße, steht das Stadtmuseum. An der Ecke der Bismarckstraße und des Kreuzwegs steht das Café Mozart. Dort arbeitet mein Vater. Er ist Kellner. Auf der anderen Seite des Kreuzwegs ist der Park. Im Park gibt es nur ein Gebäude, das Parkcafé. Gegenüber dem Café ist die Eichendorffstraße, eine Sackgasse, die zum Krankenhaus führt. Meine Mutter arbeitet im Krankenhaus.

TIME LINES

This can be used in connection with texts concerned with daily routines, stages on a journey giving times of arrival and departure, a biography, or, at a much more advanced level, with a newspaper article. Pupils set out the events in chronological order.

Lundi, 21 mai
10h

Jeudi, 24 mai
14h30

Samedi, 26 mai
12h

DERIVING ONE TEXT FROM ANOTHER

Here, pupils take a descriptive or narrative text in which some connected items of information are given. Instead of noting them on a grid (see p10), pupils present them in a different, but well-defined and familiar text type, for instance:

● From a text giving personal details, complete an identity form as if you were the young person described.

● Given a narrative text on a visit to a restaurant, deduce the 85 franc menu, and set it out on a (decorated?) pro-forma.

● From a narrative about a stay in a hotel, complete the reservation form for the author/person or people concerned.

● From an account of a Belgian child's school day, fill in his or her timetable for Monday and Tuesday, on a prepared blank timetable.

● From a narrative, complete a lost property form as if you had been the author or person concerned.

In all these cases, the pupil needs to understand a lot of the base texts and to know how the second text type (the timetable or form) works, but the information can be lifted - or deduced - from the text and the pupil does not need to make linguistic adjustments to complete the activity. When such adjustments are required, the activity is better considered as reading to write (see Chapter 4).

THE LINGUISTIC TRAWL

We have already discussed one kind of classification on p10; the intention there was to afford the learner the chance to approach that which he or she is trying to learn from a different angle. It is quite easy to focus, for example, on sets of lexical items, and to invite pupils to read and re-read a number of related texts and extract these sets, e.g. all the sports mentioned, all the foods, all non-alcoholic drinks (again, this is an active process: *is this drink alcoholic or not?* is the recurrent question), and so on. Clearly, the trawl is not limited to nouns; by reading some narrative texts and looking for those words and expressions which take the narrative forward, or tell us when things occurred, the students have a better chance of observing a narrative framework. They could collect expressions such as *d'abord, ensuite, puis alors, après, cinq minutes plus tard, et finalement, longtemps après...* Such a set will be very useful if and when the pupils want to produce a narrative of their own.

It may even be worth setting exercises which directly address such sets and which aim to help the learner differentiate and retain them. The not-so-able reader, secure in the knowledge that *Jacques va au café* means Jacques goes to the café, is quite likely to interpret *Jacques va rarement au café* and even *Jacques ne va jamais au café* as having the same meaning. Would the following kind of exercise help such readers?

Régularité

Put these people in order, with the one who is most often to be seen in the café at the top, and the one who is there least, if at all, at the bottom:

☐ *Jacques va rarement au café*

☐ *Jean va au café une fois par mois.*

☐ *Jerôme ne va jamais au café.*

☐ *Jérémie va au café deux fois par semaine.*

☐ *Jean-Paul va au café tous les soirs.*

☐ *Jules va au café presque tous les jours.*

☐ *Jim ne va presque jamais au café.*

4. Reading to write

In this chapter, we are working towards the learners' own productive use of language, assuming that their writing in the foreign language fits along this continuum:

A Writing to learn	B Writing to a model	C Learning to write
Activities such as copy writing, note taking, gap filling which are intended to support learning.	Activities such as adapting a model text, working from one text type to another (may be one line, two lines, a paragraph or a page).	Activities such as creating texts of their own suited to purpose and audience (may be one line, two lines, paragraphs or pages).

The activities which follow explore ways in which learners can be helped to move towards writing to express their own ideas and feelings, at whatever stage and age they are. On their way from A to C, learners need models; without them, their only starting point is bound to be an attempt to translate their ideas from their mother tongue; they will find it difficult to describe their cat, write about their bedroom, report an incident in the street or compose a fairy story, unless they have read some examples previously and have some idea of what such texts look like in the foreign language. While working on a model text, students can be asked to tackle a range of activities which will help them both to acquire useful structures and sentence patterns, and to look closely at how such texts hang together. The model may be no more than a single sentence; it might extend to a substantial narrative.

VERS LA CRÉATIVITÉ

When pupils are trying to see what works in the language and what doesn't, it is helpful for them if there are clear constraints on both the task and the language required.

As a warm-up activity with a year 7 class, you might write up a single sentence and invite pupils to alter individual elements and therefore the meaning of the original, thus:

Frédéric Moreau est mécanicien à Déville could become:
Pierre Moreau est pompiste à Dieppe.
Pierre Laval est garagiste à Dinan, etc.

You can add extra challenges to keep them on their toes, in this instance restricting suggestions perhaps to names beginning with P (*Pierre Parrain est plombier à Poitiers*) or occupations to do with transport, and so on. More advanced students can cope with more variables:

Georges a passé ses vacances dans un hôtel en Ecosse could become:
Paul a passé un weekend dans un appartement au bord de la mer.

FROM SENTENCE TO PARAGRAPH

Learners often need help in seeing how to combine items of information in writing so that their ideas are clearly and logically expressed.

In this example, the starting point is a single sentence and constraints of language and structure are clear. Pupils try to expand the sentence to include as much information as possible.

Challenge: How much can they include before the sentence becomes unmanageable?

For instance:

Tutor talk	Student response	Tutor action
Pierre habite Pourville		Writes '*Pierre habite Pourville*' on the board
Nom de famille?	*Pierre Plon habite Pourville.*	Writes '*Pierre Plon habite Pourville*' on the board
Type de domicile?	*Pierre Plon habite un appartement à Pourville.*	Writes '*Pierre Plon habite un appartement à Pourville*'.
Frères et sœurs? etc...	*Pierre Plon habite un appartement à Pourville et il a deux frères et une sœur.*	Writes '*Pierre Plon habite un appartement à Pourville et il a deux frères et une sœur*' on the board.

With year 10, if they are working on accidents and the like, they might take as their *point de départ* a sentence like:

Un jeune homme a failli tuer une femme.

The prompts will be things such as *participants, lieu, heure, conséquences...* and may lead to a paragraph such as:

Un jeune homme, Phillipe Leroux, a failli tuer une femme hier, quand son vélosolex est entré en collision avec elle. L'incident s'est produit Place de la Cathédrale vers 14h.

The same prompts could be used to build a paragraph based on sentences like these:

Un passant a sauvé un touriste.
Un chien a attaqué un enfant, etc.

SENTENCE STEMS

Pupils complete sentences of which they are given the beginning: they learn the possibilities and limitations of patterns they have been learning. They could start with:

Je suis...
Mon père est...

This can be done individually or as a class activity, collecting ideas on the board. What might a year 7 pupil suggest?

Je suis grand, anglais, en retard...
Mon père est boucher, strict, petit... regarder la télé...

The last suggestion, based on an English pattern, could open up a discussion about why it is not possible to complete the sentence in this way.

DESCRIPTIONS WITH 'CHARACTER'

Chapter 3 on reading to learn has already mentioned the notion of character (p13). Pupils can be asked to write short descriptions which take the character into account and to develop him in contexts with which they are becoming familiar. Taking the snobby Guillaume and having worked on clothes vocabulary, students might be asked to write an answer to the question: *Comment est-il habillé, Guillaume?* Or having done some work on hobbies: *Les loisirs de Guillaume? Et ceux de sa sœur?*

LE DIALOGUE DES MAIS

Pupils, like the rest of us, will be familiar with the 'yes but...' kind of argument, which can be used to good effect to encourage creativity in single sentences and to revise or learn ways of presenting pros and cons, in well-known situations.

Let us take the example of two holiday-makers discussing the relative merits of their campsite:

Il y avait une piscine.   *Oui, mais sa femme était affreuse!*
Oui, mais l'eau était froide!   *Ce n'était pas cher.*
Le gardien était gentil.   *Oui, mais...*

The two speakers can easily grow into characters, the moaner and the optimist, who can reappear in a number of settings, e.g. in discussions of reactions to a restaurant, a hotel, a range of trades and professions.

A LOVER'S KNOT

Pupils build a story within a tight framework. This passage is adapted from a French book for children.

Pierre aime Aurélie,
Mais Aurélie ne l'aime pas.
Elle aime le grand Bernard,
Mais Bernard ne l'aime pas.
Il préfère Suzette qui a un VTT superbe,
Mais elle ne l'aime pas.
Elle préfère Geoffroi, champion de tennis,
Mais Geoffroi n'aime pas Suzette:
Il préfère Aurélie, qui aime le grand Bernard.

Using this as a model, students could create texts of their own, perhaps supported by boxes like these, from each of which they choose one item (and not at random as you can see).

Marcel aime Marie
Georges adore Suzanne
Alice aime Martin

mais il ne l'aime pas
mais elle ne l'aime pas
mais il la déteste
mais elle le déteste

il aime
elle aime
il préfère
elle préfère

amateur de boxe
champion de tennis
très sympa
un beau chien noir
joue bien au foot
fait de la danse

Bertrand, qui a
Marie, qui est
Elise, qui a
Thomas, qui est
Alain, qui
Claire, qui

One of the important skills in story telling is to be able to relate the events in a logical sequence, and to do this learners need to be able to recognise and use time markers - words and expressions like *one day, then, after a while*.

You don't always have to **start** with a model text which pupils use as a springboard for writing. One possible approach is to lead them carefully into the narration, using their suggestions for language within a teacher-controlled framework, at least initially, e.g.:

Vous allez créer un épisode de feuilleton. A la fin, il doit y avoir des points de suspension. Le titre, c'est Un rendez-vous manqué. *Le personnage principal...*

... s'appelle comment?	*... moyen de transport?*
... est parti à quelle heure?	*... est arrivé à quelle heure?*
... quel jour?	*... a fait quoi?*
... avait rendez-vous avec qui?	*... Et soudain...?*
... où cela?	

Having created their episode, as a class, in pairs or alone, in talk or in writing, students could now be given a text of the same kind, prepared using a text manipulation package, so that they become ever more familiar with the kind of structure and narrative language involved, e.g.:

> *Jeudi soir vers sept heures, Jean-Luc a pris un billet de cinquante francs et il est parti en ville. Il avait rendez-vous avec sa copine Suzette au café de la Victoire. Au bout d'un certain temps l'autobus est arrivé et dix minutes plus tard il est descendu en ville. Puis il a traversé la rue principale pour se rendre au café. Une fois dans le café, Jean-Luc s'est assis près du flipper. Ensuite il a commandé une menthe à l'eau. Il a regardé sa montre, il était déjà sept heures quarante. Suzette est en retard... ce n'est pas normal! Pendant une demi-heure il a patienté doucement. Enfin il s'est levé pour aller au téléphone. Soudain quelqu'un lui a tapé sur l'épaule. Jean-Luc s'est retourné. Vous êtes Jean-Luc Bridieau?, a demandé l'inconnu. Oui. Alors, j'ai un message pour vous...*

NARRATIVE AND DIALOGUE

Stories often rely on the interplay between dialogue and narrative, and many pupils find the switch between them troublesome. One way of highlighting some of the different language functions within a story is to write a simple narrative version beneath boxes which contain talking heads or line drawings with empty speech bubbles. Having worked through the content of the story, pupils can be invited to fill the speech bubbles with relevant questions, answers, statements, etc. More able learners can be encouraged to try the activity the other way round, either recalling the narrative by looking only at the completed speech bubbles, or starting from a similar but different set of pictures.

Je m'appelle Jean Luard et je suis mécanicien dans un garage Renault.

Un jour, une petite VW est arrivée, et s'est arrêtée devant une pompe à essence. Je suis sorti du kiosque, et je suis allé à la voiture.

Une jeune dame était au volant. Elle a commandé 100fr. de super.

J'ai essuyé le pare-brise, et elle m'a demandé de vérifier l'huile.

J'ai ouvert le capot, et ... il y avait beaucoup de provisions, une roue de rechange, mais pas de moteur! J'étais stupéfait!

Alors, je suis allé ouvrir le coffre ... mais pas de moteur!

Puis, j'ai remarqué qu'elle avait un petit sourire aux lèvres, et j'ai compris!

J'étais le sujet d'une de ces farces, où on prend des gens en vidéo, en train de faire des bêtises ... Vous m'avez vu à la télé?

GUIDED STORY TELLING

Once learners are able to cope with longer texts, and have some idea of how to construct a story in the foreign language, there are many ways of guiding them into story telling both orally and in writing.

Giving learners the beginnings or ends of stories, for instance, can allow them to recycle and give a new context to some already familiar language. We might give pupils in year 11 or above the following opening and invite them to write a few sentences, sketching in a likely scenario:

Samstag war ein wunderschöner Tag; Sonntag aber war ganz anders.

There is an opportunity here, for example, to re-use language from a topic on leisure, daily routine or school. In this instance pupils can narrate their story without moving backwards and forwards in time, and therefore without the complications of the pluperfect.

If we take an opening such as: *Margrit hatte viel mit Stefan mitgemacht, aber jetzt hatte sie genug,* then the demands on the students are greater, both linguistically and psychologically. Filling in the background to this story may well involve shifts in time and reported speech, as well as the ability to take on a certain psychological set. We need to be aware of these demands as some opening lines can disguise a minefield of problems for the students.

Alternatively, we can give students the last line of a story and invite them to write the lead up to it: *J'ai rougi, mais il n'y avait rien à faire et je suis reparti bien vite!* Most students can think of a suitably embarrassing moment for this one!

WRITING TO A RECIPE

Stories which have to be written to a formula and have at least some predictable characters can offer just the right balance between security and challenge for the language learner. Dreams, fairy stories and ghost stories are three such examples.

Dreams nearly always involve the writer in talking about what was going on when..., an ideal opportunity for practising in French the imperfect tense. The second important ingredient is that things are never what they seem. The best way of introducing this idea to students is to have them read some short examples and re-tell them in class, perhaps from notes or symbols, so that they begin to distinguish between what is continuous and what is momentary. They can also illustrate the dreams as a forerunner to writing their own if they wish. If they are struggling to remember a dream of their own, they can always try to reproduce part of one of the original examples from memory. A group of year 10 students in a Leicester school produced their dreams and illustrations in book form, which allowed plenty of practice in drafting and re-drafting!

We have already mentioned fairy stories as a vehicle for practising narration. Students can also be encouraged to write their own with the aid of a suitable framework or recipe, such as this one, adapted from an idea by François Weiss:

1. *Tu choisis et tu décris le personnage qui va être le héros ou l'héroïne de ton conte: un prince, une princesse, un pauvre paysan, etc.*

2. *Tu imagines un but pour ton héros/ton héroïne: trouver l'amour et le mariage, devenir sage, récupérer un trésor perdu ou volé, etc.*

3. *Tu racontes comment il/elle reçoit de bons conseils: de la part d'une fée, d'un sorcier, dans un rêve, etc.*

4. *Tu décris le départ vers l'aventure.*

5. *En cours de route, il/elle rencontre un(e) ami(e) à qui il/elle rend service: une fée, un animal, un domestique, une vieille femme, etc.*

6. *Tu imagines des obstacles auxquels le héros/l'héroïne doit faire face: des brigands, des monstres, des falaises, un torrent...*

7. *L'héroïne/le héros arrive enfin. Elle/il arrive à sa destination (une île, un château, une planète...*

8. *C'est ici que vit l'adversaire; tu le décris: un ogre, une reine maligne, des monstres...*

9. *Tu expliques comment le héros/l'héroïne dompte l'adversaire (reçoit-il/elle l'aide de la part de quelqu'un?).*

10. *Fin de l'histoire - heureuse!*

A similar recipe can be provided for ghost stories.

POETRY

Writing to a pattern has been a constant theme through this chapter and, before leaving it, we should look briefly at how this can work with poetry as well as prose. Here are just a few ideas to start with, inspired by work from pupils in Leicestershire and elsewhere.

As with previous attempts at creative writing, it is always best to start by showing the pupils some examples.

In the early stages of poetry writing, simply listing words or phrases and giving them an unexpected twist at the end can work well.

Year 7 pupils could be asked to make a list of food that they might eat or drink, and to give their list an unexpected end.

> *Je mange des sandwichs,*
> *Je bois du coca,*
> *Je mange des pommes,*
> *Je bois de la limonade,*
> *Je mange des chips,*
> *Je bois du lait,*
> *Je mange des steaks,*
> *Je bois de la bière,*
> *Je m'appelle Boris,*
> *Je suis tout petit...*
> *Pour un éléphant!*

Sports and pastimes also offer plenty of scope:

> *Je joue au golf,*
> *Je joue au tennis,*
> *Je joue aux cartes,*
> *Je fais des courses en voiture,*
> *Je fais de la moto,*
> *Je fais de l'athlétisme,*
> *J'ai 9 ans et j'adore les jeux vidéo!*

As with the *Dialogue des mais* (p24), simple contrasts provide a good framework:

> *Chouette, j'ai une soirée de libre! - Mince, je n'ai pas d'argent!*
> *Chouette, plus qu'un cours, et les classes sont finies! -*
> *Mince, c'est un cours de français!*

In German, the equivalent might be *Schade - Klasse.*

Students may gradually become aware that the division between poetry and prose is not watertight, as in this student example:

> *Il fait un temps superbe,*
> *et il y a beaucoup de gens*
> *qui sont assis au soleil.*
> *Puis il fait humide*
> *et les nuages sont formés.*
> *Dans un instant il y a un orage.*
> *Tous les gens*
> *cherchent un abri contre l'orage.*
> *Après un moment les nuages ont disparu*
> *aussi vite qu'ils étaient arrivés.*
> *Il fait un temps superbe,*
> *et il y a beaucoup de gens*
> *qui sont assis au soleil.*

Was gut ist?

Gut ist wenn man etwas Erfolg hat.
Wenn man etwas gut gemacht hat.
Wenn man sich stolz fühlen kann.
Besser ist wenn man unter fallendem Schnee steht.
Wenn man in einem grünen Feld steht.
Wenn man eins mit der Welt ist.
Am besten ist wenn man Freunde zum Heiraten einladet.
Wenn man eine schöne Gattin hat.
Wenn man Liebe fühlt.

Poetry can afford students intensive practice of particular language forms. In these last three examples from sixth form German classes, patterns, lists and the repeated use of certain language forms combine to give a view of what is good in life, Monday mornings, and finally... love.

Liebe

Angeschaut
Weggeschaut
Angeschaut
Gelächelt
Zusammengekommen
Gesprochen
Gelacht
Geküsst
Wiedergetroffen
Wiedergeküsst
Geliebt.

Montag Morgen

Montag Morgen halb sieben,
Tief schlafen, laut schnarchen,
WECKER KLINGELN!
Anfangen, aufwachen, gähnen, einschlafen,
Aufwachen, aufstehen, Uhr angucken, Panik haben.
Sich duschen, sich rasieren...
*   (zu schnell, sich schneiden!)*
Frühstücken, Zeitung lesen,
Alles Quatsch.
Tasche packen, Haus verlassen,
Ohne Schlüssel...
Ach mein Gott!

A last word about text: we are not suggesting that you write all your own! There is a wealth of text available in books, newspapers and magazines. Some may well need adapting for particular groups, and even more so if you want to use it for particular purposes. The knack is to spot that which is exploitable in given texts, and to devise tasks which further that exploitation.

Here is a pen-friend letter and so
activities are not all suitable for all g
with the difficult parts of a grid, f
pupils; or some pupils taking on o
more straightforward activity.

We are **not** suggesting that you shou
the intention is to provide, over time.

Time line (1)

Mark on a calendar time line the birthdays of Sandrine, her sister and brother, and Isobel. Some deduction is necessary - if the less able pupils can't cope with that part, I could fill in that information on a prepared time line, and they could find the rest.

Time line (2)

Mark on the same line Sandrine's holidays - departure and return - and your own holiday plans.

Text manipulation

If I write a reply to Sandrine's letter, I could store it in jumbled form on disk and pupils, using block movements, could put it in logical order.

Fill the grid

If I provide a grid, or help my pupils to make one, they could give a fuller picture than on the time line, e.g.:

Personne	Age	Signe du zodiaque
Isobel		
Sandrine		
Michel		
Marie-France		
Toi		
Ton/ta partenaire		

(They will probably need to look up some of the star signs, so I need to make these available.)

The phonetic code

Some of my pupils think that *semaine* rhymes with *demain*; I could provide a list of words for them to read aloud and spot the odd one out (e.g. *main, pain, chaîne, Alain*), or a list in which they pick out 'rhymes' (e.g. *aînée, main, Ghislaine, Alain, mois, semaine, moi, année*), etc.

Spri

Pupils use the completed time li
and to ask about their classmate
relevant question forms: *Tu as d*
quand? Tu reviens quand? or th

Chére Isobel,

Merci beaucoup pour
lettre une carte pour
Tu sais, le 14 juillet e
- c'est la fête nationa
anniversaire?

Tu sais, tu es plus âg
Mon frère Michel a s
noël, et ma sœur (Ma
Elle est verseau, et m

Chaque année, pour
vacances. Cette anné
dans le Midi. Nous al
environs de Carpentr
après le grand 'rush'.

Je te souhaite donc de
heureux anniversaire.

Gros bisous,

Sandrine

Sp

I could write a few sentences for
sense, either in relation to the ba
subjects as the letter, e.g.:

Le frère de Sandrine a deux sœu
Sandrine est née en été, comme s

Moi, je n'ai ni frères ni sœurs. Je
zodiaque est gémeaux. Mon frère

s of uses you might consider. The
ne cases, they might be differentiated,
already completed for the less able
ler tasks while their classmates do a

range of activities with any one text;
xt, task and outcome.

lking

rd to talk about their holidays
need to teach/revise the
acances? Tu vas où? Tu pars

ins à cette petite
re, le quatorze juillet.
important pour nous
vas-tu fêter ton

un mois exactement!
e trois jours avant la
t née le deux février.

ire, je suis en
s pour trois semaines
camping dans les
ons le trois août,

nces et un très

nse

read and see whether they make
their own, all on the same

mois de mai, et mon signe du
anniversaire, c'est le 25 juillet.

Springboard for talking (2)

Use the completed time lines to ask six classmates about birthdays and star signs: report back so that a graph can be made of the whole class's details.

Spot the difference

If I provide another text, with 'errors' of information in it, my pupils could note the differences. This text could be word processed, and they could correct the errors and print off their corrected version.

Patterns

If they are going to talk with any flexibility about holiday plans, they need to be able to handle some parts of *aller* and *partir*. We could play with sentences like:

Mireille va à Montargis.
Christophe va à Carpentras.
(Moi) je vais à Jumièges.
Mon frère va à Fréjus, etc.

and:

Moi je pars le premier juillet. Et toi? Et ton frère? etc

Write a reply

My ablest pupils could write a reply to Sandrine's letter, as if the letter had been addressed to them. Or they could write on behalf of Isobel, in which case they will need cues to provide information about her holiday plans, her brother's birthday, etc. They might draft their efforts on the word processor.

Bande dessinée

Pupils use the story to draw a strip cartoon to represent the steps in the narrative, and perhaps fill thought and speech bubbles for the two characters; the completed strip cartoon can then be used as an aide-memoire for pupils to re-tell the story, without the original.

Linguistic trawl

Will it help my pupils to learn, if they gather all the expressions in the text(s) which have to do with moments in time? Or could they draw up a list of verbs which take the narrative forward?

le 18 mai, dix-huit heures quinze, à ce moment-là, sur ce...

Elle s'est mise à..., il a pénétré, il s'est aperçu, il l'a ouvert, etc.

Mapping: Cluedo

If I provide my pupils with a plan of the house, they could mark on it the point of entry of the burglar, where Madame Schlub was at the time... With a second account of the incident, they could do the same with that one, which would help them to spot some of the differences between the reports. Or I could devise a sort of Cluedo grid, with:

Pièce:

Meuble:

Arme:

Délit:

Prediction

With a very bright group, if I rub out the punch line (*C'est pour le téléphone*) before they see the text, they might be able to predict what it might be; then we could brainstorm all we have thought of; the idea is not to 'get it right' so much as to have them read the text very carefully, and 'create' something within a constrained framework.

Merci madame! ???
C'est tout ce que vous avez? ???
C'est le mark que votre mari me doit! ???

Patterns

Which of the sentence patterns might be of most help to my pupils? What are the grammatical implications, when we put it to use? How can we practise it?

Il a pris le sac et en a sorti un mark.
J'ai pris le/la... et j'en ai sorti...
Elle... le/la... et elle en a... etc

34

Here is a text - the story is true, but
activities suggested are not all suita
differentiated, with the ablest (for ex
only part of it; or the ablest completir
words.

This text might be suitable for the
suggesting that you should use the
intention is to provide variety of text,

Un camb

Madame Maria Sch
Bielefeld (Allemagn
d'un choc sévère. V
attendait tranquille
Volker, 44 ans. A 1
le repas du soir. C'
cambrioleur a péné
fenêtre de la terrass
pas fermée. Pensan
rentrait, Madame S
dans le salon. Mais
n'était pas son mar
foulard, et habillé t
d'un revolver. Mad
l'intrus l'a fait taire
suite est à peine cro
aperçu du sac à ma
canapé. Il s'en est s
mark.

Voilà, a-t-il dit, c'e

Et sur ce, il a pris l
sauvé en sortant pa

Le tout avait duré t
Le M

It might help my pupils to read th
forma for them to complete:

Qui? _____
Où? _____
Quand? _____
Suite des événements? _____
1 _____
2 _____
3 _____
4 _____
Conclusion? _____

pted from a German newspaper. The
oups. In some cases, they might be
g in the whole grid, and the less able
activity in sentences, the less able in

ar 10 or sixth formers. We are **not**
of activities with any one text; the
come.

rdinaire

omiciliée à
n de se remettre
er, 18 mai, elle
de son mari,
t mise à preparer
nt-là qu'un
aison par la porte-
e Schlub n'avait
on mari qui
à sa rencontre
venait de rentrer
squé par un
ntrus était muni
poussé un cri, et
nt son arme. La
brioleur s'est
Schlub sur le
, en a sorti un

phone.

onnaie et s'est
être.

Metz

Spot the difference

If I provide a second account (my assistant could write it, if we
have one this term), in the same style but with the kinds of
differences which actually appear in newspapers, my pupils could
find the differences and note them. If I tell them that there are (say)
five, that would help them; if I say there are at least four, that is
crueller, but might encourage even more readings! Instead of a
second written text, the assistant could make a news broadcast
with the same story, and pupils could again spot the differences.

*Madame Maria Schlub, 44 ans, domiciliée à Bielefeld
(Allemagne), est en train de se remettre d'un choc considérable.
Vendredi dernier (18 mai), vers dix-huit heures, elle était dans la
salle de bains...*

Dialogue

A springboard for talk. When her husband came home, Madame
Schlub must have told him all about it; he asked questions. Could my
pupils, in pairs or as a class exercise, 'find' this dialogue? Or they, as
Madame Schlub, might telephone a friend. Could I help them by
providing the questions, and perhaps the occasional stage direction?

Mais comment est-il entré dans la maison?

Elle n'était pas fermée à clé? etc

Dialogue: your witness

Another possible springboard for talk. Pupils take the part of the
woman, the burglar, the husband, or a policeman doing the
interrogating... perhaps I should do the questioning? This
contrasts in tone with the 'informal' dialogues...

Vous êtes donc... ?
Vous habitez où?
Le soir en question, vous étiez toute seule à la maison? etc

Text manipulation

When pupils have understood the text, I could put it - or a
similar one - into a text manipulation package, and they could
do a range of familiarisation activities on the computers. No
access to the computer suite? Perhaps I could cut up this text or
another manually, into half-sentences, and my pupils could work
in pairs to (re)construct it.

lly if I provide a grid or pro-

_____
_____
_____
_____
_____
_____